A HUMOROUS LOOK AT
LOVE & Marriage

Compiled by
BOB PHILLIPS

HARVEST HOUSE PUBLISHERS
Eugene, Oregon 97402

A HUMOROUS LOOK AT LOVE AND MARRIAGE

Copyright © 1981 by Harvest House Publishers
Eugene, Oregon 97402

Library of Congress Catalog Card Number 80-83841
ISBN 0-89081-268-3

Printed in the United States of America.

A Humorous Look
At Love and Marriage

Contents

· 1 ·

Cupid's Arrows

When Cupid aims for the mark, he usually Mrs. it.

☆   ☆   ☆

It's the glancing shot by Cupid, the one that barely nicks you, that causes the most suffering.

☆   ☆   ☆

There is evidence that Cupid is a trapper as well as a hunter.

☆   ☆   ☆

Cupid's darts hurt more coming out than going in.

☆   ☆   ☆

Someone once said that Cupid is a lifesaver, but that's ridiculous! He pushes you right into the Sea of Matrimony.

☆   ☆   ☆

Brad: "I hear Cupid almost got you last week."
Charlie: "Yes, I had an arrow escape."

☆   ☆   ☆

- 2 -

Boy Meets Girl

He: "Here is your engagement ring."
She: "But this diamond has a flaw in it."
He: "You shouldn't notice that; we are in love, and love is blind."
She: "Not stone blind."

☆   ☆   ☆

Jean: "When are you thinking about getting married?"
Joan: "Constantly."

☆   ☆   ☆

He: "What can I say that will convince you of my love and cause you to marry me?"
She: "Only three little words."

He: "Yes, and what are they?"
She: "One million dollars."

☆   ☆   ☆

Guy: "Hello, Lisa, do you still love me?"
Gal: "Lisa? My name is Roberta."
Guy: "I'm so sorry—I keep thinking this is Thursday."

☆   ☆   ☆

Harry: "My girlfriend has a huge lower lip, but I don't mind."
Gary: "You don't?"
Harry: "No, her upper lip covers it."

☆   ☆   ☆

Melba: "Men are all alike."
Pam: "Men are all I like, too."

☆   ☆   ☆

Pam: "Were you nervous when George proposed?"
Linda: "No, dear, that's when I stopped being nervous."

☆   ☆   ☆

Girl: "Whenever I look at you, I'm reminded of a famous man."

Boy: "You flatter me. Who was the
          man?"

Girl: "Darwin."

☆   ☆   ☆

Mary: "Well, what happened when you
          showed the girls in the office your
          new engagement ring? Did they all
          admire it?"

Sara: "Better than that—four of them
          recognized it!"

☆   ☆   ☆

Boy: "Meet me at the Waldorf-Astoria at
          eight."

Girl: "The Waldorf? Say, that's a nice
          place."

Boy: "Yeah, and it's close to where we're
          going, too."

☆   ☆   ☆

Guy: "Margie, I love you! I love you,
          Margie!"

Gal: "In the first place, you don't love
          me; and in the second place, my
          name isn't Margie."

☆   ☆   ☆

Becky: "Do you love me with all your heart
          and soul?"

Dave: "Uh-huh."

Becky: "Do you think I'm the most beautiful girl in the world?"
Dave: "Uh-huh."
Becky: "Do you think my lips are like rose petals?"
Dave: "Uh-huh."
Becky: "Oh, you say the most beautiful things."

☆   ☆   ☆

She prays every night: "Dear Lord, I don't ask a thing for myself. Just send my parents a son-in-law."

☆   ☆   ☆

"I've been asked to get married lots of times."
"Who asked you?"
"Mother and Father."

☆   ☆   ☆

She: "You remind me of Don Juan."
He: (Flattered) "Tell me just how."
She: "Well, for one thing, he's been dead for years."

☆   ☆   ☆

He: "What would you say if I asked you to marry me?"
She: "Nothing. I can't talk and laugh at the same time."

☆　　　☆　　　☆

In the spring a young man's fancy lightly turns to what the girls have been seriously thinking of all winter.

☆　　　☆　　　☆

"No, he hasn't sprung the question yet, but his voice sure has an engagement ring in it."

☆　　　☆　　　☆

Q:　　　A man who always remembers a woman's birthday but forgets her age is called what?

A:　　　A smart man.

☆　　　☆　　　☆

She:　　　"Do you know why I won't marry you?"

He:　　　"I can't think."

She:　　　"You guessed it right away."

☆　　　☆　　　☆

Con-　　　"I can tell just by looking into a
ceited:　　　girl's eyes exactly how she feels about me."

Girl:　　　"Gee, that must be embarrassing for you."

☆　　　☆　　　☆

Him: "There is one word that will make me the happiest man in the world. Will you marry me?"
Her: "No!"
Him: "That's the word!"

☆   ☆   ☆

Frances: "So Tom and you are to be married? Why, I thought it was a mere flirtation."
Melba: "So did Tom."

☆   ☆   ☆

"He thinks no woman is good enough for him."
"He may be right."
"He may be left."

☆   ☆   ☆

Boy: "You look prettier every minute. Do you know what that is a sign of?"
Girl: "Yes, you are about to run out of gas."

☆   ☆   ☆

Helen: "I hear he proposed and you accepted. Did he tell you that he had proposed to me first?"
Karen: "No, but he did mention that he had done a lot of foolish things before we met."

☆　　　☆　　　☆

Boy:　　"I would like to marry you."
Girl:　　"Well, leave your name and address, and if nothing better turns up, I will notify you."

☆　　　☆　　　☆

She:　　"You finally asked Daddy for my hand in marriage. What did he say?"
He:　　"Not a word. He just fell on my neck and sobbed."

☆　　　☆　　　☆

She wears a diamond ring that reminds her of the capital of Arkansas—Little Rock.

☆　　　☆　　　☆

Q:　　What do they call a fellow who introduces his best girl to his best friend?
A:　　An idiot.

☆　　　☆　　　☆

Lisa:　　"My fiance has been telling everybody that he is going to marry the most beautiful girl in the world."
Chris:　　"Oh, what a shame! And after all the time you've been going with him."

☆   ☆   ☆

"Is it true, Miss Elderleigh, that you are going to be married soon?"
"Well, no, it isn't, but I am very grateful for that rumor."

☆   ☆   ☆

She was going to have an announcement party, but the engagement was broken, so she went ahead and called it a narrow-escape party.

☆   ☆   ☆

She: "If I refuse to be your wife, will you really commit suicide?"
He: "That has been my usual procedure."

☆   ☆   ☆

He: "Honey, would you say I'm built like a Greek god?"
She: "No, I'd say you were built more like a Greek restaurant."

☆   ☆   ☆

Two young lovers were trying to find a spot to be alone while they had a long embrace. They were unable to find a secluded area, so they decided to go to the railway station where they could pretend they were kissing goodbye. A porter who watched them for a period of time came up and said, "Why don't you take her around to the bus terminal? They go every three minutes from there."

☆   ☆   ☆

Boy: "Will you marry me?"
Girl: "No, but I'll always admire your
          good taste."

☆   ☆   ☆

Joan: "George is just crazy about me."
Jill: "Don't take too much credit to
          yourself. He was crazy before you
          ever met him."

☆   ☆   ☆

"My girlfriend takes advantage of me."
"What do you mean?"
"I invited her out to dinner and she asked me if
she could bring a date."

☆   ☆   ☆

Jay: "I have half a mind to get
          married."
Bill: "That's all you need."

☆   ☆   ☆

Boy: "You could learn to love me,
          couldn't you?"
Girl: "Well, I learned to eat spinach."

☆   ☆   ☆

"When I went out with Fred, I had to slap his face five times."
"Was he that fresh?"
"No! I thought he was dead."

☆ ☆ ☆

He: "It's a funny thing, but every time I dance with you, the dances seem very short."

She: "They are. My fiance is leader of the orchestra."

☆ ☆ ☆

Girl: "Did you kiss me when the lights were out?"

Boy: "No!"

Girl: "It must have been that fellow over there!"

Boy: (Starting to get up) "I'll teach him a thing or two!"

Girl: "You couldn't teach him a thing!"

☆ ☆ ☆

Father: "When I was your age, I never kissed a girl. Will you be able to tell your children that?"

Son: "Not with a straight face."

☆ ☆ ☆

Martha: "I don't intend to be married until

after I'm 30.''

Barbara: ''And I don't intend to be 30 until after I'm married.''

☆   ☆   ☆

Son: ''How do they catch lunatics, Dad?''
Dad: ''With lipstick, beautiful dresses, and pretty smiles.''

☆   ☆   ☆

Mother: ''If a young man asks you for a kiss, refuse it.''
Daughter: ''And if he doesn't ask for it?''

☆   ☆   ☆

Girl: ''Would you like to take a walk?''
Boy: ''I'd love to.''
Girl: ''Well, don't let me detain you.''

☆   ☆   ☆

She: ''What's your opinion of these women who imitate men?''
He: ''They're idiots.''
She: ''Then the imitation is successful.''

☆   ☆   ☆

The matchmaker was selling the girl to the man: ''Have I got a girl for you—she comes with a dowry of $100,000.'' He said, ''Sounds good. I'd like to see her picture.'' The matchmaker said, ''Sorry, but with a $100,000 dowry I never show pictures.''

☆   ☆   ☆

Boy: ''If you refuse to me mine, I'll hurl myself over that 500-foot cliff over there.''

Girl: ''That's a lot of bluff.''

☆   ☆   ☆

Guy: ''I'm a lady killer.''

Gal: ''Yeah, they take one look at you and drop dead.''

☆   ☆   ☆

Little girl: (To bride at wedding reception) ''You don't look nearly as tired as I should have thought.''

Bride: ''Don't I, dear? But why did you think I should look tired?''

Little girl: ''Well, I heard mom and dad say that you'd been running after Mr. McKee for months and months.''

☆   ☆   ☆

Rich: ''So you loved and lost?''

Glen: ''On the contrary, I came out a winner.''

Rich: ''How was that?''

Glen: ''She returned my presents and

accidentally put in some of another fellow's.''

☆　　　　☆　　　　☆

He: "If you would give me your phone number, I would give you a call."

She: "It's in the book."

He: "Good. What's your name?"

She: "It's in the book, too."

☆　　　　☆　　　　☆

He: "Do you think your father would object to my marrying you?"

She: "I don't know; if he's anything like me, he would."

☆　　　　☆　　　　☆

Boy: (With one hand cupped over the other) "If you can guess what I have in my hand, I'll take you out tonight."

Girl: "An elephant."

Boy: "Nope! But that's close enough. I'll pick you up at 7:30."

☆　　　　☆　　　　☆

Son: "Why is a man not allowed to have more than one wife?"

Father: "Because the law protects those who are incapable of protecting themselves."

☆   ☆   ☆

Gary: "She said I was interesting and brave."

Lowell: "You could never marry a woman who deceived you from the start."

☆   ☆   ☆

Boy: "You know, sweetheart, since I met you I can't eat, I can't sleep, I can't drink—"

Girl: "Why not?"

Boy: "I'm broke!"

☆   ☆   ☆

Woman: "Oh, Mr. Policeman! Mr. Policeman! A man is following me, and I think he's crazy!"

Policeman: "I agree."

☆   ☆   ☆

David: "And where is your sister, Jimmy?"

Jimmy: "She just ran upstairs to change rings when she saw you coming."

☆   ☆   ☆

After a blind date a fellow said to his friend,

"After I got home last night, I felt a lump in my throat." "You really like her, huh?" "No, she's a karate expert."

☆　　　　☆　　　　☆

"Why does my sweetheart always close her eyes when I kiss her?"
"Look in the mirror, and you'll know."

☆　　　　☆　　　　☆

"Dear Emily, words cannot express how much I regret having broken off our engagement. Will you please come back to me? Your absence leaves a space no one can fill. Please forgive me and let us start all over again. I need you so much. Yours forever, Bob.
P.S. By the way, congratulations on winning the sweepstake."

☆　　　　☆　　　　☆

"Without you everything is dark and dreary. The clouds gather and the wind beats the rain. Then comes the warm sun—you are like a rainbow."
"Is this a proposal or a weather report?"

☆　　　　☆　　　　☆

"How come you go steady with Eloise?"
"She's different from other girls."
"How so?"
"She's the only girl who will go with me."

☆   ☆   ☆

Amy: "What made you quarrel with
         Conrad?"
Sue: "Well, he proposed to me again last
         night."
Amy: "Where was the harm in that?"
Sue: "My dear, I had accepted him the
         night before."

☆   ☆   ☆

Boy: "Ah, look at the cow and the calf
         rubbing noses in the pasture. That
         sight makes me want to do the
         same."
Girl: "Well, go ahead—it's your cow."

☆   ☆   ☆

"If you refuse to marry me, I'll die," said the
young romantic. And sure enough, 50 years later
he died.

☆   ☆   ☆

The young lady eyed her escort with great disap-
proval. "That's the fourth time you've gone
back for more ice cream and cake, Wilbert," she
said acidly. "Doesn't it embarrass you at all?"
"Why should it?" the hungry fellow shrugged.
"I keep telling them I'm getting it for you."

☆   ☆   ☆

Girl: "Do you love me?"
Boy: "Yes, dear."
Girl: "Would you die for me?"
Boy: "No—mine is an undying love."

☆   ☆   ☆

Boy: "Darling, I've lost all my money. I haven't a cent in the world."
Girl: "That won't make any difference, dear. I'll love you just as much, even if I never see you again."

☆   ☆   ☆

"Bill told me I was the only girl he ever loved."
"Doesn't he say it beautifully?"

☆   ☆   ☆

Friend: "Are you the bridegroom?"
Young man: "No, sir. I was eliminated in the semifinals."

☆   ☆   ☆

He: "Will you love me when I'm old?"
Her: "I will love you. I will cherish the ground you walk upon. I will . . . you won't look like your father, will you?"

☆   ☆   ☆

Boy: "You look like a sensible girl; let's
            get married."
Girl: "Nothing doing. I'm just as sensible
            as I look."

☆   ☆   ☆

Girl: "The man I marry must stand out in
            company, be musical, tell jokes,
            sing, dance, and stay at home
            nights."
Mother: "You don't want a husband—
            you want a TV set."

☆   ☆   ☆

"I just had a date with a pair of Siamese twins."
"Did you have a good time?"
"Yes and no."

☆   ☆   ☆

Boy: "Why won't you marry me? Is there
            someone else?"
Girl: "There must be."

☆   ☆   ☆

One girl to another: "There's never a dull moment when you're out with Wilbur—it lasts the
whole evening."

☆   ☆   ☆

She: "My father takes things apart to see
        why they don't go."
He: "So what?"
She: "So you'd better go."

☆   ☆   ☆

1st   "What would you do if you had
Coed: five dates with the same man and he
        never tried to kiss you?"
2nd   "I would do what everyone else
Coed: does—I'd lie about it."

☆   ☆   ☆

A ring on the hand is worth two in the voice.

☆   ☆   ☆

On a lonely, moonlit, country road the car
engine coughed and the car came to a halt. Then
the following conversation took place:
"That's funny," said the young man. "I wonder
what that knocking was?"
"Well, I can tell you one thing for sure," the
girl answered icily. "It wasn't opportunity."

☆   ☆   ☆

Boy: "Please whisper those three little
        words that will make me walk on
        air."
Girl: "Go hang yourself."

☆   ☆   ☆

Boy: "No woman ever made me look
          stupid!"
Girl: "Who did, then?"

☆   ☆   ☆

Did you hear about the young man who lost his
girlfriend? He wanted to send his girlfriend a
rose for every year of her life on her birthday.
The florist made a mistake and sent 31 roses instead of 21.

☆   ☆   ☆

The young woman looked back to smile sweetly
at the waiting line at the telephone booth. "I
won't be long—I just want to hang up on him."

☆   ☆   ☆

One of the unmarried girls who works in a busy
office arrived early the other morning and began
passing out cigars and candy, both tied with
blue ribbons. When asked what the occasion
was, she proudly displayed a diamond solitaire
on her third finger, left hand, and announced:
"It's a boy . . . six feet tall and 187 pounds."

☆   ☆   ☆

- 3 -

Old Maids

An old maid is a girl who knows all the answers, but no one ever asks her the question.

☆   ☆   ☆

Optimistic bachelor: "Let's get married!"
Pessimistic spinster: "Good heavens! Who'd have us?"

☆   ☆   ☆

Spinster—the most singular of women.

☆   ☆   ☆

Old maid—a lady in waiting.

☆ ☆ ☆

Lady-in-waiting—the feminine of bachelor.

☆ ☆ ☆

Just as Hopkins and widow Jones started up the aisle to the altar, every light in the church went out.
What did they do then?
They kept right on going. The widow knew the way.

☆ ☆ ☆

Joe: "They tell me your spinster died quite happily."
Pete: "Yes—somebody told her marriages are made in heaven."

☆ ☆ ☆

Bill: "Why is Miss Jones wearing black?"
Sue: "She is in mourning for her husband."
Bill: "Why, she never had a husband!"
Sue: "No, that is why she mourns."

☆ ☆ ☆

Becky: "Hi, Margie. Joan and Marsha and I were just talking about you. We were wondering why you never married. Did you ever have the chance to marry?"

Margie: "Suppose you ask your husbands."

☆   ☆   ☆

Old maid: girl with a wait problem.

☆   ☆   ☆

Old maid's laughter—he! he! he!

☆   ☆   ☆

A minister forgot the name of the couple he was going to marry, so he said from the pulpit, "Will those wishing to be united in holy matrimony please come forward after the service."
After the service, 13 old maids came forward.

☆   ☆   ☆

- 4 -

Bachelors

A bachelor is one who never Mrs. a girl.

☆   ☆   ☆

A bachelor is a man who believes that one can live as cheaply as two.

☆   ☆   ☆

A bachelor is a fellow who doesn't have anyone to share the troubles he doesn't have.

☆   ☆   ☆

A bachelor is a man who can be miss-led only so far.

☆   ☆   ☆

Q: What is a bachelor?
A: A man who thinks before he acts and
        then doesn't act.

☆   ☆   ☆

A bachelor is a man who never makes the same
mistake once.

☆   ☆   ☆

A bachelor is a man who can take a nap on top
of the bedspread.

☆   ☆   ☆

A bachelor is a man who prefers to cook his own
goose.

☆   ☆   ☆

A bachelor is a fellow who believes it is much
better to have loved and lost than to have to get
up for the 2 a.m. feeding.

☆   ☆   ☆

A bachelor is someone who thinks that the only
thoroughly justified marriage was the one that
produced him.

☆   ☆   ☆

What a pity that nobody knows how to manage

a wife except a bachelor!

☆   ☆   ☆

Not all men are fools; some are bachelors.

☆   ☆   ☆

Bachelors know more about women than married men do; that's why they're bachelors.

☆   ☆   ☆

Mike: "What do you call a man who's been lucky in love?"
Joe: "A bachelor."

☆   ☆   ☆

A bachelor told his friend: "I'm going to make my will out and divide it equally among the four ladies who refused my proposal of marriage."
"Why do that?" said the friend.
"Because," replied the bachelor, "I owe all my earthly happiness to them."

☆   ☆   ☆

A bachelor is a man who lost the opportunity of making some woman miserable.

☆   ☆   ☆

- 5 -

True Love

Love—perpetual emotion.

☆　　　　☆　　　　☆

Love—the only fire against which there is no insurance.

☆　　　　☆　　　　☆

Love—a heartburn.

☆　　　　☆　　　　☆

Love—a heart attack.

☆　　　　☆　　　　☆

Love—a disease like the measles; it's all the

worse when it comes late in life.

☆   ☆   ☆

Love—the softening of the hearteries.

☆   ☆   ☆

Love—an island of emotion entirely surrounded by expenses.

☆   ☆   ☆

Love makes fools wits, and wits fools.

☆   ☆   ☆

Love quickens all the senses—except common sense.

☆   ☆   ☆

Love doesn't really make the world go round. It just makes people dizzy.

☆   ☆   ☆

Love may be blind, but it seems to be able to find its way around in the dark.

☆   ☆   ☆

Life is just one fool thing after another. Love is just two fool things after each other.

☆ ☆ ☆

Love is like an onion: you taste with delight, and when it's gone, you wonder whatever made you bite!

☆ ☆ ☆

Love is sometimes like a poisoned mushroom. You can't tell if it's the real thing until it's too late.

☆ ☆ ☆

Love is something different from delirium, but it's hard to tell the difference.

☆ ☆ ☆

Love is a three-ring circus—engagement ring, wedding ring, and suffer-ring.

☆ ☆ ☆

There's only one cure for a man in love, and that's a good dose of marriage. If that doesn't cure him, nothing will.

☆ ☆ ☆

The cure for love at first sight: second sight.

☆ ☆ ☆

Puppy love—the beginning of a dog's life.

☆ ☆ ☆

Better to have loved a short man than never to have loved a tall.

☆ ☆ ☆

Do you believe in love at first sight? Well, I think it saves a lot of time.

☆ ☆ ☆

- 6 -

Kissing

Kissing shortens life—single life.

☆ ☆ ☆

A kiss is the shortest distance between two.

☆ ☆ ☆

In kissing, two heads are better than one.

☆ ☆ ☆

It depends on the girl whether stealing a kiss is petty larceny or simply grand.

☆ ☆ ☆

Kissing—a means for getting two people so close

together that they can't see anything wrong with
each other.

☆   ☆   ☆

Q: What flowers are kissable?
A: Tulips.

☆   ☆   ☆

There may be a few girls who've never been
kissed, but there are mighty few who have been
kissed only once.

☆   ☆   ☆

Never let a fool kiss you and never let a kiss
fool you.

☆   ☆   ☆

Girl: "I'm telling you for the last
            time—you can't kiss me."
Boy: "Oh, I knew you would weaken."

☆   ☆   ☆

He: "I promise you, the next time you
            contradict me, I'm going to kiss
            you."
She: "Oh, no you're not!"
Him: "If I tried to kiss you, would you
            call for help?"
Her: "Do you need help?"

☆　　　　☆　　　　☆

You can't kiss a girl unexpectedly—only sooner than she thought you would.

☆　　　　☆　　　　☆

"May I kiss you?"
Silence.
"May I please kiss you?"
Silence.
"Are you deaf?"
"No, are you paralyzed?"

☆　　　　☆　　　　☆

Rick:　　"Your little brother just saw me kiss you. What can I give him to keep him from telling?"
Linda:　"He generally gets a dollar."

☆　　　　☆　　　　☆

He:　　"They say kisses are the language of love."
She:　　"Well, why don't you say something?"

☆　　　　☆　　　　☆

Romance is kissing your girlfriend on the eyes. Reality is getting her false eyelashes caught in your teeth.

☆   ☆   ☆

Mother: "Louise, your hair is all mussed up. Did that young man kiss you against your will?"

Louise: "He thinks he did, Mother."

☆   ☆   ☆

He: (with hands over her eyes) "If you can't guess who it is in three guesses, I'm going to kiss you."

She: "Jack Frost, Davy Jones, Santa Claus."

☆   ☆   ☆

He: "Sweetheart, if I'd known that tunnel was so long, I'd have given you a kiss."

She: "Gracious! Wasn't that you?"

☆   ☆   ☆

Girl: "And are mine the only lips you have kissed?"

Boy: "Yes, and they are the sweetest of all."

☆   ☆   ☆

Boy: "Boy, if I had a nickel for every girl I'd kissed—"

Girl: "You'd be able to buy a pack of gum."

☆　　　☆　　　☆

Husband: "If a man steals anything, he will live to regret it."

Wife: "You used to steal kisses from me before we were married."

Husband: "That's right."

☆　　　☆　　　☆

Boy: "I want to be honest. You're not the first girl I've kissed."

Girl: "I want to be honest. You've got a lot to learn."

☆　　　☆　　　☆

- 7 -

Wedding Plans

A wedding is where the bride looks stunning and the groom looks stunned.

☆　　　☆　　　☆

Nancy:　　"A bride wears white as a symbol of happiness, for her wedding day is the most joyful day of her life."

Buck:　　"And why do men wear black?"

☆　　　☆　　　☆

Shotgun wedding—where you get married for better or hearse.

☆　　　☆　　　☆

Bride:　　"I don't want to forget any insignificant details."

Mother:　"Don't worry! I'll be sure he's there."

☆　　　☆　　　☆

Roy:　"But you promised at the altar to obey me."

Patty:　"Of course. I didn't want to make a scene."

☆　　　☆　　　☆

Did you hear about the married man who ran his wedding movies backwards? He wanted to remember what it was like to be a free man.

☆　　　☆　　　☆

"I hear the bride ran away from the altar."
"Lost her nerve, I suppose?"
"No, found it again."

☆　　　☆　　　☆

Don:　"Do you think it's unlucky to postpone a wedding?"

Rich:　"Not if you keep on doing it."

☆　　　☆　　　☆

Barb:　"I want to congratulate you. This is one of the happiest days of your life."

Sally:　"But I'm not getting married until tomorrow."

Barb: "That's why I say today is one of
          your happiest days."

☆   ☆   ☆

The problem with all these teenage marriages is
that they don't last long. One teenage marriage
broke up so fast that they were fighting over
who gets custody of the acne.

☆   ☆   ☆

It's easy to tell a teenage wedding: the people
don't throw rice—they throw Tootsie-Rolls!

☆   ☆   ☆

- 8 -

Marriage Defined

Marriage is when a man gets hooked on his own line.

☆ ☆ ☆

Modern marriage is like a cafeteria—a woman grabs what she wants and pays for it later.

☆ ☆ ☆

Marriage is nature's way of keeping people from fighting with strangers.

☆ ☆ ☆

Marriage is like twirling a baton, turning handsprings, or eating with chopsticks—it looks so easy till you try it.

☆ ☆ ☆

Marriage is like a prize fight—the preliminaries are generally better than the main event.

☆   ☆   ☆

Marriage is like a midnight phone call—you get a ring and then you wake up.

☆   ☆   ☆

Marriage is like the army—everyone complains, but you'd be surprised at how many reeinlist.

☆   ☆   ☆

Marriage is called the Sea of Matrimony because it's so hard to keep your head above water.

☆   ☆   ☆

Marriage is like a railroad sign—first you stop, then you look, then you listen.

☆   ☆   ☆

Marriage is like a bathtub—once you are in it for awhile, it's not so hot.

☆   ☆   ☆

Marriage is an institution that turns a night owl into a homing pigeon.

☆   ☆   ☆

Marriage is a great institution, but I'm not ready

for an institution yet.

☆   ☆   ☆

Marriage is an institution of learning in which a man loses his bachelor's degree and his wife acquires a master's.

☆   ☆   ☆

Marriage teaches you loyalty, forbearance, self-restraint, and a lot of other qualities you wouldn't need if you'd stayed single.

☆   ☆   ☆

Marriage is a legalized method of suppressing freedom of speech.

☆   ☆   ☆

Being married is like any other job. It helps a lot if you like the boss.

☆   ☆   ☆

A marriage certificate is a legal paper that lets guys keep the game in captivity after the hunting season is over.

☆   ☆   ☆

To marry a woman for her beauty is like buying a house for its paint.

Marriage resembles a detective story—it's full of surprises, and you never know just how it's going to turn out.

☆ ☆ ☆

Statistics prove that marriage is a preventive against suicide.
And statistics also prove that suicide is a preventive against marriage.

☆ ☆ ☆

Love is blind, and marriage is an eye-opener.

☆ ☆ ☆

A man never knows what real happiness is until he gets married, and then it's too late.

☆ ☆ ☆

Married men live longer than single men, or at least they complain more about it.

☆ ☆ ☆

A married man lives longer than a single man, or maybe it only seems longer.

☆ ☆ ☆

There are two things that cause unhappy marriages—men and women.

☆ ☆ ☆

A deaf husband and a blind wife are always a happy couple.

☆ ☆ ☆

Marriage is that part of a girl's life that comes between the lipstick and the broomstick.

☆ ☆ ☆

A man is incomplete until he's married, and then he's finished.

☆ ☆ ☆

Keep your eyes open before marriage and half-shut afterward.

☆ ☆ ☆

Marriage is the alliance of two people, one of whom never remembers birthdays and the other who never forgets them.

☆ ☆ ☆

When we are married or dead, it's for a long time.

☆   ☆   ☆

Before marriage, a man declares that he will be boss in his home or know the reason why; after marriage he knows the reason why.

☆   ☆   ☆

Marriages are like diets—they can be ruined by having a little dish on the side.

☆   ☆   ☆

The cooing usually stops when the honeymoon is over, but the billing goes on forever.

☆   ☆   ☆

The difficulty with marriage is that we fall in love with a personality, but must live with a character.

☆   ☆   ☆

Before marriage a man yearns for a woman. After marriage, the "y" is silent.

☆   ☆   ☆

It takes two to make a marriage—a young girl and an anxious mother.

☆   ☆   ☆

Matrimony was probably the first union to defy management.

☆   ☆   ☆

Marriage is like a violin—after the music stops, the strings are still attached.

☆   ☆   ☆

A happy marriage is when a couple is as deeply in love as they are in debt.

☆   ☆   ☆

- 9 -

The Ideal Wife

WHAT EVERY MAN EXPECTS—

Always beautiful and cheerful. Could have married movie stars, but wanted only you.
Hair that never needs curlers or beauty shops.
Beauty that won't run in a rainstorm.
Never sick—just allergic to jewelry and fur coats.
Insists that moving the furniture by herself is good for her figure.
Expert in cooking, cleaning house, fixing the car or TV, painting the house, and keeping quiet.
Favorite hobbies: mowing the lawn and shoveling snow.
Hates charge cards.
Her favorite expression: "What can I do for you, dear?"

Thinks you have Einstein's brain but look
like Mr. America.
Wishes you would go out with the boys so
she could get some sewing done.
Loves you because you're so sexy.

WHAT HE GETS

She speaks 140 words a minute with gusts
up to 180.
She once was a model for a totem pole.
A light eater—as soon as it gets light, she
starts eating
Where there's smoke, there she is—
cooking.
She lets you know you only have two
faults—everything you say and everything
you do.
No matter what she does with it, her hair
looks like an explosion in a steel-wool
factory.
If you get lost, open your wallet—she'll find
you.

☆   ☆   ☆

- 10 -

The Ideal Husband

WHAT EVERY WOMAN EXPECTS—

He will be a brilliant conversationalist.
A very sensitive man—kind and understanding, truly loving.
A very hard-working man.
A man who helps around the house by washing dishes, vacuuming floors, and taking care of the yard.
Someone who helps his wife raise the children.
A man of emotional and physical strength.
A man who is smart as Einstein, but looks like Robert Redford.

WHAT SHE GETS—

He always takes her to the best restaurants.
Someday he may even take her inside.

He doesn't have any ulcers—he gives them.
Anytime he gets an idea in his head, he has
the whole thing in a nutshell.
He's well-known as a miracle worker—it's
a miracle when he works.
He supports his wife in the manner to
which she was accustomed—he's letting her
keep her job.
He's such a bore that he even bores you to
death when he gives you a compliment.
He has occasional flashes of silence that
make his conversation brilliant.

☆   ☆   ☆

· 11 ·

My Wife

My wife is the sweetest, most tolerant, most beautiful woman in the world. This is a paid political announcement.

☆   ☆   ☆

1st Husband:	"I think my wife is getting tired of me."
2nd Husband:	"What makes you feel that way?"
1st Husband:	"She keeps wrapping my lunches in road maps."

☆   ☆   ☆

Golfer: "Pardon me, but would you mind if I played through? I've just heard that my wife has been taken seriously ill."

☆   ☆   ☆

"What did you give your wife for Christmas last year?"
"A cemetery plot!"
"What are you going to give her this year?"
"Nothing. She didn't use last year's gift."

☆   ☆   ☆

"My wife said she wouldn't talk to me for 30 days."
"Why should that make you sad?"
"Today is her last day."

☆   ☆   ☆

"I try to do everything to make my wife happy. She complained about the housework so I bought her an electic iron, an electric dishwasher, and an electric dryer. Then she complained that there were so many gadgets around the house she had no room to sit down. What could I do?"
"Buy her an electric chair."

☆   ☆   ☆

"My wife says if I don't chuck golf, she'll leave me."
"That's too bad."
"Yes, I'll miss her."

☆   ☆   ☆

Jim: "It's no disgrace to work."
Tim: "That's what I tell my wife."

☆   ☆   ☆

"My wife is very irritable. The least thing sets her off."
"You're lucky at that—mine's a self-starter."

☆   ☆   ☆

I told my wife I'd buy her a mink coat when man walked on the moon—my luck!

☆   ☆   ☆

My wife suffers in silence louder than anyone I know.

☆   ☆   ☆

Talk about an exciting weekend—yesterday my wife and I were standing in front of a wishing well, and she fell in! I didn't realize those things worked!

☆   ☆   ☆

"Does your wife like housework?"
"She likes to do nothing better."

☆   ☆   ☆

I think the romance has gone out of our

marriage. My wife just sent me a 25th anniversary card. It was addressed to Occupant.

☆ ☆ ☆

My wife and I cooperate wonderfully whenever we're out in the car together. She drives while I steer.

☆ ☆ ☆

"How long did it take your wife to learn to drive?"
"About 2½ cars."

☆ ☆ ☆

He: "My wife just got a ticket for
            speeding."
Him: "That's nothing! My wife is so bad
            the police gave her a season ticket."

☆ ☆ ☆

One thing I'll say for my wife, she's a very neat housekeeper. If I drop my socks on the floor, she picks them up. If I throw my clothes around, she hangs them up. I got up at 3 o'clock the other morning and went in the kitchen to get a glass of orange juice. I came back and found the bed made.

☆ ☆ ☆

"Does a rabbit's foot really bring good luck?"
"I should say so. My wife felt one in my money
pocket once and thought it was a mouse."

My wife will never find where I hid my extra
money. I hid it in my socks that need mending!

"My wife kisses me only when she needs
money."
"Don't you think that's often enough?"

My wife just had plastic surgery—I took away
all her credit cards.

You have no idea the way my wife shops. She
doesn't even have a charge card anymore. All
she has to do is see a sale, and the goose bumps
rise up in the shape of her credit number.

The way my wife looks in the morning! She ran
after the garbage man and said, "Am I too late
for the garbage?"
He said, "No, jump in."

☆ ☆ ☆

My wife is just as beautiful today as when I married her. Of course, it takes her longer.

☆ ☆ ☆

My wife spends a fortune on cold creams and oils—puts them all over her body. I went to grab her, but she slid out of the bed.

☆ ☆ ☆

They say brunettes have a sweeter disposition than blondes and redheads. Don't believe it! My wife has been all three, and I couldn't see any difference.

☆ ☆ ☆

"Every once in a while my wife puts on one of those mud packs."
"Does it improve her looks?"
"Only for a few days—then the mud falls off."

☆ ☆ ☆

My wife is something. She never lies about her age. She just tells everyone she's as old as I am. Then she lies about my age.

☆ ☆ ☆

My wife spent four hours in the beauty shop the

other day, and that was just for the estimate.

☆   ☆   ☆

"Have you and your wife ever had any difference of opinion?"
"Yes, but she didn't know it."

☆   ☆   ☆

"Do you think I'm going to wear this old squirrel coat all my life?"
"Why not, dear? The squirrels do."

☆   ☆   ☆

Son: "Do you know, dad, my Sunday school teacher says that in some parts of Africa a man doesn't know his wife until he marries her?"
Dad: "Why single out Africa?"

☆   ☆   ☆

"I was sorry for your wife in church this morning when she had a terrific attack of coughing and everyone turned to look at her."
"You needn't worry about that. She was wearing a new spring hat."

☆   ☆   ☆

"I'm afraid the mountain air would disagree with me."

"My dear, it wouldn't dare!"

☆   ☆   ☆

I think I'm losing my mind, but my wife told me it's impossible, because she says I never had one.

☆   ☆   ☆

She's an angel—always up in the air and harping on something.

☆   ☆   ☆

"My wife is always asking for money," complained a man to his friend. "Last week she wanted $200. The day before yesterday she asked me for $125. This morning she wanted $150."
"That's crazy," said the friend. "What does she do with it all?"
"I don't know," said the man. "I never give her any."

☆   ☆   ☆

"Would you mind compelling me to move on, officer? I've been waiting on this corner three hours for my wife."

☆   ☆   ☆

What every man needs is a little support, a little

encouragement. I don't mind going off every morning into the rat race, but I just wish my wife wouldn't bet on the rats!

☆　　　　☆　　　　☆

My wife talks to her plants for three hours every day. I once asked a geranium, "How do you stand it?" The geranium replied, "Who listens?"

☆　　　　☆　　　　☆

I came home last night, and there was a car in the dining room.
I said to my wife, "How did you get the car in the dining room?"
She said, "It was easy. I made a left turn when I came out of the kitchen."

☆　　　　☆　　　　☆

"My wife always has the last word."
"You're lucky. Mine never gets to it."

☆　　　　☆　　　　☆

"The doctor told my wife she should take some exercises."
"And is she doing it?"
"If jumping to conclusions and running up bills can be called exercise."

☆　　　　☆　　　　☆

Nobody can cook like my wife, Joan, but they came pretty close to it when I was in the Army.

☆   ☆   ☆

When my wife wants something, she uses a sign language. She always signs for this and signs for that.

☆   ☆   ☆

"My wife has been using a flesh-reducing roller for nearly two months."
"And can you see any result yet?"
"Yes—the roller is much thinner."

☆   ☆   ☆

- 12 -

My Husband

Husband: "Sweetheart, I love you terribly."
Wife: "You certainly do."

☆   ☆   ☆

"Does your husband ever remember your
wedding anniversary?"
"No, so I remind him of it in January and June,
and get two presents."

☆   ☆   ☆

He: "I wonder why women pay more at-
         tention to beauty than they do to
         brains."
She: "Because no matter how stupid a
         man is, he is seldom blind."

☆   ☆   ☆

Husband: "What have you ever done to benefit
           your fellowman?"
Wife: "I married you, didn't I?"

☆   ☆   ☆

Betty: "Does your husband ever take
           advice?"
Sue: "Occasionally, when nobody is
           looking."

☆   ☆   ☆

Becky: "Hello, dear. How's the pain in the
           neck?"
Pam: "He's out golfing."

☆   ☆   ☆

Husband: "Why isn't dinner ready?"
Wife: "Oh, I've been downtown bargain
           hunting all afternoon and I just
           couldn't get home in time."
Husband: "Huh! Like all women—looking for
           something for nothing, I suppose?"
Wife: "Yes, indeed. Trying to get you a
           birthday present."

☆   ☆   ☆

"When you quarreled today, you let your husband have the last word. That was not usual."

"No, but I wanted to give him a little pleasure—it's his birthday."

☆   ☆   ☆

"Don't you ever look at a man and wish you were single again?"
"Yes."
"Who?"
"My husband."

☆   ☆   ☆

Husband: "I gave you the best years of my life."
Wife: "Those were the best?"

☆   ☆   ☆

The shivering wife in the rowboat was saying to her husband, who was fishing: "Tell me again how much fun we're having—I keep forgetting."

☆   ☆   ☆

First Eskimo wife: "Does your husband stay out late during the winter nights?"
Second Eskimo wife: "Why, last night he didn't get home till half-past January."

☆   ☆   ☆

He: "You don't deserve a husband like me."
She: "I don't deserve sinus trouble, either, but I have it."

"Did you ever catch your husband flirting?"
"Yes; that's the very way I did catch him."

☆   ☆   ☆

Wife to husband: "This year let's give each other practical gifts like socks and fur coats."

☆   ☆   ☆

When she asks him a question, she has to take a lot for grunted.

☆   ☆   ☆

Wife: "Dear, could I have some spending money?"

Husband: "Money, money, money. If you ask me, I think you need brains more than you need money."

Wife: "I was just asking you for what I thought you had the most of."

☆   ☆   ☆

Husband: "What have you been doing with all the grocery money I gave you?"

Wife: "Turn sideways and look in the mirror."

☆   ☆   ☆

Husband: "Why do you weep and sniffle over a

	TV program and the imaginary woes of people you have never met?''
Wife:	''For the same reason you scream and yell when a man you don't know makes a touchdown.''

☆   ☆   ☆

Sharon:	''Is your husband tight with money?''
Esther:	''Is he! Every time he takes a penny out of his pocket, Lincoln blinks at the light.''

☆   ☆   ☆

''My husband just ran off with someone else. I can hardly control myself.''

''Go ahead and let go, dearie. You'll feel better after a good laugh.''

☆   ☆   ☆

Melba:	''My husband was named Man of the Year.''
Pam:	''Well, that shows you what kind of a year it's been.''

☆   ☆   ☆

My husband really embarrassed me the other day in a restaurant. When he drank his soup, six couples got up and started to dance.

☆   ☆   ☆

Wife I: "Does your husband have ulcers?"
Wife II: "No, but he's a carrier!"

☆   ☆   ☆

There is one thing bigger than my husband's
stomach—his appetite.

☆   ☆   ☆

Husband: "I just lost ten pounds!"
Wife: "Turn around; I think I found
            them."

☆   ☆   ☆

(Wife to husband who just got off the scale):
"Your fortune says that you are handsome,
chivalrous, and wealthy. It even has your weight
wrong!"

☆   ☆   ☆

Ken: "I slept like a log."
Melba: "Yes, I heard the sawmill."

☆   ☆   ☆

Husband: "I'd like to know whatever became
            of the old-fashioned girls who fainted
            when a man kissed them."
Wife: "What I'd like to know is what hap-
            pened to the old-fashioned men who
            made them faint."

☆ ☆ ☆

"My husband didn't leave a bit of insurance."
"Then where did you get that gorgeous diamond ring?"
"Well, he left $1000 for his casket and $5000 for a stone. This is the stone."

☆ ☆ ☆

To give you an idea of how lazy my husband is, he wouldn't even help move his mother-in-law out of his house.

☆ ☆ ☆

She thought she was getting a model husband, but he's not a working model.

☆ ☆ ☆

She keeps asking her husband to show her his birth certificate. She wants proof that he's alive.

☆ ☆ ☆

She avoids getting up with a grouch. She rises before he does.

☆ ☆ ☆

"I hear your husband is a linguist."
"Yes, he speaks three languages—golf, football, and baseball."

☆   ☆   ☆

My husband has three moods—hungry, thirsty or both.

☆   ☆   ☆

My husband is on a seafood diet. Every time he sees food, he eats.

☆   ☆   ☆

My husband's greatest labor-saving device: tomorrow.

☆   ☆   ☆

My husband is a do-it-yourself man. Every time I ask him to do something, he says, "Do it yourself."

☆   ☆   ☆

Husband: "This report says that every time I breathe, three Chinese people die."
Wife: "That doesn't surprise me."

☆   ☆   ☆

Husband: "I know you're having a lot of trouble with the baby, dear, but keep in mind, 'The hand that rocks the cradle is the hand that rules the world'."

Wife: "How about you taking over the
          world for a few hours while I go
          shopping?"

☆   ☆   ☆

Police-   "In the gun battle a bullet struck my
man: head and went into space."
Wife: "Well, at least you're honest."

☆   ☆   ☆

"Did he take his misfortunes like a man?"
"Precisely. He laid the blame on his wife."

☆   ☆   ☆

They were married for better or for worse. He
couldn't have done better, and she could have
done worse.

☆   ☆   ☆

- 13 -

In a Stew

Newlywed husband: "Do you mean to say
there's only one course for dinner
tonight? Just cheese?"

Bride: "Yes, dear. You see, when the chops
caught fire and fell into the dessert, I
had to use the soup to put it out."

☆   ☆   ☆

A sorely pressed newlywed husband tried
valiantly to console his little bride, who
sprawled, dissolved in tears, on the chaise
lounge. "Darling," he implored, "believe me. I
never said you were a terrible cook. I merely
pointed out that our garbage disposal has
developed an ulcer."

☆   ☆   ☆

Newlywed couples shouldn't expect the first few meals to be perfect. After all, it takes time to find the right restaurant.

☆   ☆   ☆

Young bride as she brings a dish for the social:
      "The two things I prepare best are meatballs and peach pie."
Young man standing near: "And which one is this?"

☆   ☆   ☆

Bob: "Somehow I don't think my wife knows her way around the kitchen."
Ray: "Why do you say that?"
Bob: "This morning I saw her trying to open an egg with a can opener."

☆   ☆   ☆

I've eaten so much frozen food that I have the only tonsils in town that are chapped.

☆   ☆   ☆

Wife: "Darling, you know that cake you asked me to bake for you? Well, the dog ate it."
Husband: "That's okay, dear; don't cry. I'll buy you another dog."

☆   ☆   ☆

Bride: "I made this pudding all by myself."
Hubby: "Splendid! But who helped you lift it out of the oven?"

☆   ☆   ☆

Husband: "Beans again!"
Wife: "I don't understand it. You liked beans on Monday, Tuesday, and Wednesday, and now all of a sudden you don't like beans."

☆   ☆   ☆

I don't want to say anything about my wife's cooking, but when she says, "Guess who's coming to dinner?" it's an ambulance.

☆   ☆   ☆

Jane: "I cooked my first meal last night—it was a grand success."
Mother: "How nice."
Jane: "Yes, he's going to get me a cook right away."

☆   ☆   ☆

Husband: "And here is an eggplant."
Wife: "When will the eggs be ripe?"

☆   ☆   ☆

- 14 -

Bigamy

Bigamy is when two rites make a wrong.

☆　　　　☆　　　　☆

Bigamist—a man who leads two wives.

☆　　　　☆　　　　☆

Bigamist—someone who makes the same mistake twice.

☆　　　　☆　　　　☆

The extreme penalty for bigamy is two mothers-in-law.

☆　　　　☆　　　　☆

Why a man wants a wife is a mystery. Why a man wants two wives is a bigamistery.

☆   ☆   ☆

Son: "I never could understand why a fellow should not be allowed to have more than one wife."

Dad: "Well, after you're married you'll realize that the law protects those who are incapable of protecting - themselves."

☆   ☆   ☆

Son: "Dad, does bigamy mean that a man has one wife too many?"

Dad: "Not necessarily, son. A man can have one wife too many and still not be a bigamist."

☆   ☆   ☆

The angry wife called on her attorney and announced she wanted to sue her husband for divorce.
"What grounds?" asked the attorney.
"Bigamy. I'll show him he can't have his Kate and Edith too."

☆   ☆   ☆

- 15 -

Wedlock or Deadlock?

The man's wife, infuriated by his laziness, remarked, "When his time is up, I won't bury him. I'll have him cremated. And when I get his ashes, I'll put them in the hourglass. He never did a lick of work all his life, but I'll have him working for me then!"

☆　　　☆　　　☆

Steward-ess:　"I'm sorry, Mr. Jones, but we left your wife behind in Chicago."

Man:　"Thank goodness! I thought I was going deaf!"

☆　　　☆　　　☆

The president of the local women's club was telling her husband of their plans to raise money for the club.

"We're going to serve as caddies-for-a-day at the country club, but don't know what to call ourselves. We've thought of Caddie-etts, and Link Lassies, but we need something more original."

"I have it," offered her husband. "How about Tee-Bags?"

☆   ☆   ☆

There are some girls who can't take a joke, while others prefer one to no husband at all.

☆   ☆   ☆

A married couple trying to live up to a snobbish lifestyle went to a party. The conversation turned to Mozart. "Absolutely brilliant, magnificent, a genius!"

The woman, wanting to join in the conversation, remarked casually, "Ah, Mozart. You're so right. I love him. Only this morning I saw him getting on the No. 5 bus going to Coney Island."

There was a sudden hush, and everyone looked at her. Her husband was shattered. He pulled her away. "We're leaving right now. Get your coat and come."

In the car as they drove home, he kept muttering to himself. Finally his wife turned to him. "You're angry about something."

"Oh, really? You noticed it?" he sneered. "My goodness! I've never been so embarrassed in my life! You saw Mozart take the No. 5 bus to

Coney Island? You idiot! Don't you know the No. 5 bus doesn't go to Coney Island?''

☆　　　　☆　　　　☆

New bride: ''When we go in the motel, let's act like we've been married for years.''
New husband: ''All right. You carry the bags.''

☆　　　　☆　　　　☆

Women are fools to marry men. On the other hand, what else is there to marry?

☆　　　　☆　　　　☆

Bob:　　　''Time separates the best of friends.''
Bill:　　　''So docs moncy.''
Ken:　　　''And don't forget marriage!''

☆　　　　☆　　　　☆

''My wife has been nursing a grouch all week.''
''Been laid up, have you?''

☆　　　　☆　　　　☆

Wife:　　　''I dreamed you gave me $100 for summer clothes last night. You wouldn't spoil that dream would you, dear?''
Husband:　''Of course not, darling. You may keep the $100.''

☆   ☆   ☆

Wife: "I think you only married me
            because my daddy left me a lot of
            money."
Husband: "That's not true. I didn't care who
            left you the money."

☆   ☆   ☆

Policeman: "How did this accident happen?"
Motorist: "My wife fell asleep in the back
            seat."

☆   ☆   ☆

Wife: "Darling, take me to the movies."
Husband: "I've already taken you to the
            movies."
Wife: "Yes, I know, but they have talkies
            now."

☆   ☆   ☆

After a serious operation a lady was still in a
coma. Her worried husband stood at the foot of
her bed. "Well," said the nurse reassuringly, "at
least age is on her side."
"She's not so young," said the husband,
"she's 45."
At this point the patient moved slightly, and
quietly but firmly murmured, "44."

☆   ☆   ☆

Ike: "I'm a man of few words."
Mike: "I'm married, too."

☆   ☆   ☆

"My wife thinks I'm perfect."
"Yes, I heard her say so."
"Did you? When?"
"The time she called you an idiot."

☆   ☆   ☆

In our marriage we made a decision never to go to bed mad. We haven't had any sleep for three weeks.

☆   ☆   ☆

A couple was celebrating their golden wedding anniversary. Their domestic tranquility had long been the talk of the town. A local newspaper reporter was inquiring as to the secret of their long and happy marriage.
"Well, it dates back to our honeymoon," explained the lady. "We visited the Grand Canyon and took a trip down to the bottom of the canyon by pack mule. We hadn't gone too far when my husband's mule stumbled. He took him by the ears, shook him vigorously and said, 'That's once.' We proceeded a little farther when the mule stumbled again. Once more my husband took him by the ears, shook him even more vigorously and said, 'That's twice.' We hadn't gone a half-mile when the mule stumbled a

third time. My husband promptly removed a revolver from his pocket and shot him. I started to protest over his treatment of the mule when he grabbed me by the ears, shook me vigorously and said, 'That's once.' ''

☆   ☆   ☆

Boy: ''Do you know, dad, that in some
            parts of Africa a man doesn't know
            his wife until he marries her?''
Dad: ''Why single out Africa?''

☆   ☆   ☆

''But you must admit that men have better judgment than women.''
''Oh, yes—you married me, and I you.''

☆   ☆   ☆

The two men entered the lavish house, and when they were alone, one of them asked:
''Was that your wife who opened the door?''
''Of course it was,'' said the other. ''You don't think I would hire a maid that ugly, do you?''

☆   ☆   ☆

''Why are you cutting up that newspaper?''
''Well, there's a story here about a man who shot his wife for going through his pockets. I'm going to put it in my pocket.''

☆   ☆   ☆

"The Lord made us beautiful and dumb."
"How's that?"
"Beautiful so men would love us, and dumb so
we could love them."

☆   ☆   ☆

A man rose from his seat in a crowded bus so a
lady standing nearby could sit down. She was so
surprised she fainted.
When she revived and sat down, she said,
"Thanks."
Then he fainted.

☆   ☆   ☆

Wife: "Did you see that hat Mrs. Jones
               wore to church?"
Husband: "No!"
Wife: "Did you see the new dress Mrs.
               Smith had on?"
Husband: "No!"
Wife: "A lot of good it does you to go to
               church!"

☆   ☆   ☆

"You seem rather hoarse this morning, Mrs.
Brown."
"Yes, my husband came home very late last
night."

☆   ☆   ☆

He: "Will you marry me?"
She: "No."
          And they lived happily ever after!

☆   ☆   ☆

Husband: "Now look, Lucy. I don't want to
          seem harsh, but your mother has
          been living with us for 20 years now.
          Don't you think it's time she got a
          place of her own?"
Wife: "My mother? I thought she was your
          your mother."

☆   ☆   ☆

He carries a picture of his children and a sound
track of his wife.

☆   ☆   ☆

Did you hear about the man who asked the
bellboy to carry his bag? The bellboy came over
and picked up his wife.

☆   ☆   ☆

"John, is it true that money talks?"
"That's what they say, my dear."
"Well, I wish you'd leave a little here to talk to
me during the day. I get so lonely."

☆   ☆   ☆

Bill: "If I had a wife like yours, I'd stay
           home every night of the week."
Bob: "I'll say you would, or get your neck
           broken."

☆   ☆   ☆

Wife: "You're lazy, you're worthless,
           you're bad-tempered, you're
           shiftless, you're a thorough liar."
Husband: "Well, my dear, no man is perfect."

☆   ☆   ☆

He suggested a settlement figure and the ad-
juster turned purple with rage.
"Mister," he exploded, "can't you see that your
claim for $50,000 for a single digit is
ridiculous?"
"Maybe you think so," he explained, "but that
was no ordinary thumb. It was the one I kept
my wife under."

☆   ☆   ☆

Jan: "Wake up, John, there's a burglar
           going through your pants pockets."
John: "Oh, you two just fight it out be-
           tween yourselves."

☆   ☆   ☆

Esther: "Why did you get rid of your waterbed?"

Sharon: "Bill and I were drifting apart."

☆   ☆   ☆

Son: "Dad, what is a weapon?"

Father: "Why, son, that's something you fight with."

Son: "Is mother your weapon?"

☆   ☆   ☆

Before they were married, she promised to knot for him. Now she needles.

☆   ☆   ☆

Boy: "Dad, I just got a part in the school play. I play the part of a man who's been married for 25 years."

Father: "That's a good start, son. Just keep at it, and one of these days you'll get a speaking part."

☆   ☆   ☆

The wife had spent the whole afternoon trying to balance her checkbook. When her husband came home, she handed him four neatly typed sheets, with items and costs in their respective columns. He read them over carefully. "Milkman, $3.25; Cleaner, $4.75; Phone bill $11.20; etc." Everything was clear except one

item reading, ''ESP, $24.49.'' Warily, he asked her, ''What does ESP mean?''
''Error some place,'' she explained.

☆　　　　☆　　　　☆

Sue:　　　''See that woman over there? She's been married four times—once to a millionaire, then to an actor, third to a minister, and last to an undertaker.''

Sal:　　　''I know! One for the money, two for the show, three to get ready, and four to go.''

☆　　　　☆　　　　☆

''Did you hear about the guy who had three wives in three months? The first two died of poisoned mushrooms.''
''What happened to the third wife?''
''She died from a blow on the head. She wouldn't eat the mushrooms!''

☆　　　　☆　　　　☆

''I understand your husband came from a fine old family.''
'' 'Came' is hardly the word—he brought it with him.''

☆　　　　☆　　　　☆

Melba:　　''I notice by this article that men

become bald much more often than
women because of the intense activity of their brains.

Ken: "Yes, and I notice that women don't
raise beards because of the intense
activity of their chins."

☆   ☆   ☆

Some people ask the secret of our long marriage.
We take time to go to a restaurant two times a
week. A little candlelight, dinner, soft music,
and a slow walk home. She goes Tuesdays; I go
Fridays.

☆   ☆   ☆

At eight o'clock I said to my wife, "Let's go out
and have a sail." At a quarter past eight we
went out. On the sea the boat capsized. We
would have drowned, but a passing dolphin let
us get on his back, and brought us safely to
land.
You smile; what do you find incredible in this
story?
"That part about your wife being ready at a
quarter past eight."

☆   ☆   ☆

Bill: "Is your wife having any success in
learning how to drive the car?"
Jay: "Well, the road is beginning to turn
when she does."

☆ ☆ ☆

Wife: Everyone in church is talking about the quarrel the Joneses have been having. Some are taking her side and some are taking his.''

Husband: ''And I suppose a few eccentric individuals are minding their own business.''

☆ ☆ ☆

Becky: (suspiciously) ''I think he plans to marry me for my money.''

Bob: ''Well, if he does, he'll have earned it.''

☆ ☆ ☆

''Dearest, is there anything in life but love?''
''Nothing whatever, my sweet. Will dinner be ready pretty soon?''

☆ ☆ ☆

''For months,'' said a women's libber, ''I couldn't imagine where my husband spent his evenings.''
''And then what happened?'' asked her friend breathlessly.
''Well,'' she said, ''one evening I went home and there he was.''

☆ ☆ ☆

He claims they're happily married. The fact is, he's happy, she's married.

☆   ☆   ☆

Every married man should forget his mistakes. There is no use two people remembering the same thing.

☆   ☆   ☆

She talks so much that she was married three years before she found out that her husband is deaf and dumb.

☆   ☆   ☆

"For once," she screamed, "I should have taken my mother's advice and never married you. How she tried to stop me!"
"Holy mackerel," he exclaimed, "How I've misjudged that woman!"

☆   ☆   ☆

They had been married just two weeks, and he was going through a batch of mail that had arrived.
"Honey," he said, "aren't these bills for clothes you bought before we were married?"
"Yes, darling," she replied. "You aren't upset about it, are you?"
"Not really," he replied, "but don't you think

it's a bit unfair to ask a fish to pay for the bait
he was caught with?''

☆ ☆ ☆

Women's Libber: ''The time will come when
    women will get men's wages.''
Husband in audience: ''How true—next
    payday.''

☆ ☆ ☆

Whatever you may think about women changing
their minds, you seldom hear of a groom being
left at the church.

☆ ☆ ☆

Son: ''What is a monologue, dad?''
Dad: ''That's a conversation between a
    man and a wife.''
Son: ''But our teacher said that was a
    dialogue.''
Dad: ''Your teacher isn't married, son.''

☆ ☆ ☆

Son: ''How much does it cost to get mar-
    ried, Dad?''
Dad: ''I don't know. I'm still paying
    on it.''

☆ ☆ ☆

He was called a model husband, so he looked up the word. He found out that it means "A small imitation of the real thing."

☆　　　　☆　　　　☆

"And do you know, I refused to marry Jim McManus a year ago, and he has been drinking ever since."
"Isn't that carrying a celebration a little too far?"

☆　　　　☆　　　　☆

We've been married 28 years, and I have recognized all my wife's faults. And she would have recognized all of mine—if I had any.

☆　　　　☆　　　　☆

A man and his wife had their first quarrel during the fiftieth year of their wedded life. The man tucked a gracious note under his wife's pillow: "My darling bride, let's put off quarreling until after the honeymoon is over. Your devoted husband."

☆　　　　☆　　　　☆

He:　　　　"Where are you going on your vacation?"
Him:　　　 "Yellowstone National Park."
He:　　　　"Don't forget Old Faithful."
Him:　　　 "She's going with me."

☆   ☆   ☆

"Your age, please?" asked the census taker.
"Well," said the woman, "let me figure it out. I was 18 when I married and my husband was 30. He is now 60, or twice as old as he was then, so I am now 36."

☆   ☆   ☆

"Ever struck by lightning?"
"After ten years of married life, I don't remember trifles like that."

☆   ☆   ☆

A wife is the only person who can look into the top drawer of a dresser and find a man's socks that aren't there.

☆   ☆   ☆

Wife: "My husband and I like the same things, but it took him 16 years to learn."

☆   ☆   ☆

Husband: (Reading the morning paper) "Another cup of coffee!"
Wife: "Aren't you going to the office today?"
Husband: "Oh, my goodness! I thought I was at the office!"

☆   ☆   ☆

Her husband's male secretary appeared at the
door, dressed in black. "I have come to inform
you that your husband is dead."
She turned pale, stifled a scream, and then
regained possession of herself.
"I'm glad you're taking it so well," said the
secretary with a sad smile. "Of course, your
husband isn't really dead."
"No?" she gasped. "Then what—"
"He lost all his money in the stock market
today, and he instructed me to break the news
to you gently."

☆   ☆   ☆

Bill: "I remember my wedding day very
          distinctly. I carried my new bride
          across the threshold of our little
          house and said, 'Honey, this is your
          and my little world."
Bob: "And I suppose you've lived happily
          ever after?"
Bill: "Well, not exactly. We've been
          fighting the World's Championship
          ever since."

☆   ☆   ☆

Ken: "I hear you advertised for a wife.
          Any replies?"
Bob: "Sure, hundreds."
Ken: "What did they say?"

Bob: "They all said, 'Here, take mine'."

☆   ☆   ☆

A man was driving an auto with his wife in the back seat when he stalled his car on the railroad tracks as the train was approaching.
His wife screamed, "Go on, go on!"
"You've been driving all day from the back seat. I've got my end across, so now see what you can do with your end."

☆   ☆   ☆

He: "I'd love to be married to you
          someday."
She: "All right. I'll put you on my
          wedding list."

☆   ☆   ☆

The only time some husbands can get a word in edgewise is when they talk in their sleep.

☆   ☆   ☆

I've been married 36 years, and I don't regret one day of it. The one unregrettable day was July 8, 1953.

☆   ☆   ☆

Wife: "Such an odd thing happened today.
          The clock fell off the wall, and if it

had fallen a moment sooner, it
would have hit mother.''
Husband: ''I always said that clock was slow.''

☆ ☆ ☆

''Were you married by the justice of the peace?''
''Yes, but they should have called him the
secretary of war.''

☆ ☆ ☆

Bad news: your wife was captured by cannibals.
Worse news: They have already eaten.

☆ ☆ ☆

Views expressed by husbands are not necessarily
those of the management.

☆ ☆ ☆

''Don't you think, dear, that a man has more
sense after he is married?''
''Yes, but it's too late then.''

☆ ☆ ☆

I just heard of a man who met his wife at a
travel bureau. She was looking for a vacation,
and he was the last resort.

☆ ☆ ☆

"Why don't Peter and Polly make up?"
"They'd like to, but unfortunately they can't remember what they quarreled about."

☆   ☆   ☆

"What happened to that dopey blonde your husband used to run around with?"
"I dyed my hair."

☆   ☆   ☆

"This is our tenth anniversary. Let's have duck for dinner."
"Why kill the duck for what happened ten years ago?"

☆   ☆   ☆

A Kansas cyclone hit a farmhouse just before dawn one morning. It lifted the roof off, picked up the beds on which the farmer and his wife slept, and set them down gently in the next county.
The wife began to cry.
"Don't be scared, Mary," her husband said. "We're not hurt."
Mary continued to cry. "I'm not scared," she responded between sobs. "I'm happy 'cause this is the first time in 14 years we've been out together."

☆   ☆   ☆

"No, Henry, I don't think a manicurist should marry a dentist."
"And why not?"
"If we fought, it would be tooth and nail."

☆   ☆   ☆

Wife: "Honey, I can't get the car started. I think it's flooded."
Husband: "Where is it?"
Wife: "In the swimming pool."
Husband: "It's flooded."

☆   ☆   ☆

"Tomorrow is our 25th wedding anniversary. What do you suggest?"
"How about two minutes of silence?"

☆   ☆   ☆

Wife: "This article on overpopulation of the world says that somewhere in the world there is a woman having a baby every four seconds!"
Husband: "I think they ought to find that woman and stop her!"

☆   ☆   ☆

Husband: "I have tickets for the theater."
Wife: "Wonderful, darling. I'll start dressing right away."

Husband: "That's a good idea. The tickets are
          for tomorrow night."

☆   ☆   ☆

"How long have you been married?" asked the
friend.
"We've been happily married for seven years,"
answered the husband, adding, "Seven out of 16
ain't bad."

☆   ☆   ☆

Rod: "So your wife is very broad-minded?"
Ron: "Yes, she believes there are always
          two sides to an argument—hers and
          her mothers."

☆   ☆   ☆

I'm for a woman president. At least a woman
wouldn't spend billions for atomic weapons and
staff. She'd shop around until she found them
on sale.

☆   ☆   ☆

A diplomat is a man who can convince his wife
she looks fat in a mink coat.

☆   ☆   ☆

Rich: "Have you ever suspected your wife
          of leading a double life?"

Glen: "Continually—her own and mine."

☆   ☆   ☆

"Bill's wife always laughs at his jokes."
"They must be pretty clever."
"No—she is."

☆   ☆   ☆

"Be an angel and let me drive."
She did, and he is.

☆   ☆   ☆

Two ladies stopped to look at a bookstore
display.
"There's a book on HOW TO TORTURE YOUR
HUSBAND," said one.
"I don't need that," the other replied. "I have a
system of my own."

☆   ☆   ☆

Wife: "If you had it to do over again,
           would you marry me, dear?"
Husband: "Of course, if I *had* to do it over
           again."

☆   ☆   ☆

She's so tired at the end of the day that she can
hardly keep her mouth open.

☆　　　　☆　　　　☆

I'll never forget the first time I put my arm around my bride-to-be. Right away I felt a lump in my throat.
She was a karate expert.

☆　　　　☆　　　　☆

She:　　　"Landing a man on the moon doesn't worry me nearly as much as landing one right here on earth."

☆　　　　☆　　　　☆

Their marriage is a partnership—he's the silent partner.

☆　　　　☆　　　　☆

The honeymoon is over when he tells her they should name a hurricane after her.

☆　　　　☆　　　　☆

I remember the day I had a wreck in my car. Six months later, I married her.

☆　　　　☆　　　　☆

You can always tell when a marriage is shaky. The partners don't even talk to each other during the television commercials.

☆   ☆   ☆

As the crowded elevator descended, Mrs. Wilson became increasingly furious with her husband, who was delighted to be pressed against a gorgeous blonde.

As the elevator stopped at the main floor, the blonde suddenly whirled, slapped Mr. Wilson and said, "That will teach you to pinch!"

Bewildered, Mr. Wilson was halfway to the parking lot with his wife when he choked, "I—I—didn't pinch that girl."

"Of course you didn't," said his wife, consolingly. "I did."

☆   ☆   ☆

Wife: "All men are fools."
Husband: "Of course, dear. We are made like that so you girls won't have to be old maids."

☆   ☆   ☆

She wishes she'd paid closer attention to the sign on the courthouse steps: "This way for marriage licenses. Watch your step."

☆   ☆   ☆

Ken: "For 18 long years my girl and I were deliriously happy."
Bob: "Then what happened?"
Ken: "We met."

☆　　　　☆　　　　☆

Intuition is that uncanny second sense that tells a woman she is absolutely right—whether she is or not.

☆　　　　☆　　　　☆

"My husband is a deceitful skunk," the woman cried to her mother. "Last night he pretended to believe me when he knew I was lying."

☆　　　　☆　　　　☆

A man sitting at his window one evening casually called to his wife: "There goes that woman Ken Roberts is in love with."

His wife in the kitchen dropped the plate she was drying, ran into the living room, knocked over a vase, and looked out the window.

"Where, where?" she said.

"Over there," said the husband. "The woman in the blue dress standing on the corner."

"Why, you big idiot," she replied, "that's his wife."

"Yes, of course," answered the husband with a satisfied grin.

☆　　　　☆　　　　☆

"We've been married for 50 years."

"How does it feel?"

"Who feels after 50 years?"

☆   ☆   ☆

Before Albert was married, he said he would be the boss or know the reason why.
And now?
He knows the reason why.

☆   ☆   ☆

The average American family consists of 4.1 persons. You have one guess as to who constitutes the .1 person.

☆   ☆   ☆

Man to travel agent: "We'd like to go on a pleasure cruise. Book us on different ships."

☆   ☆   ☆

Ken: "Does your husband have a den?"
Melba: "He doesn't need one. He just growls all over the house."

☆   ☆   ☆

· 16 ·

Definitions

Acrimony—another name for marriage.

☆   ☆   ☆

Alimony—the high cost of leaving.

☆   ☆   ☆

Alimony—taxation without representation.

☆   ☆   ☆

Alimony—the marital version of "Fly now, pay later."

☆   ☆   ☆

Alimony—Bounty from the mutiny.

☆ ☆ ☆

Ambitious wife—the power behind the drone.

☆ ☆ ☆

Amiss—someone who is not married.

☆ ☆ ☆

Anniversaries—when a husband may forget the past, but had better not forget the present.

☆ ☆ ☆

Bagdad—what mother did when she met father.

☆ ☆ ☆

Blind date—when you expect to meet a vision, and she turns out to be a sight.

☆ ☆ ☆

Bridegroom—a thing they have at weddings.

☆ ☆ ☆

Bridegroom—the proof that a woman can take a joke.

☆ ☆ ☆

Chivalry—attitude of a man toward someone else's wife.

☆ ☆ ☆

Diamond jubilee—when the last installment is paid on the engagement ring.

☆ ☆ ☆

Elliptical—the feel of a kiss.

☆ ☆ ☆

Engagement ring—a tourniquet applied to the third finger of a girl's left hand to stop circulation.

☆ ☆ ☆

Experienced married man—one who can tell when he and his wife come to the end of one argument and begin another.

☆ ☆ ☆

Flirt—a hit-and-run lover.

☆ ☆ ☆

Flirting—the gentle art of making a man feel pleased with himself.

☆ ☆ ☆

Frau—many a man lives by the sweat of his frau.

☆　　　　☆　　　　☆

Futile remark—the one a man makes for the purpose of changing the subject when the wife complains because he has forgotten their wedding anniversary or her birthday.

☆　　　　☆　　　　☆

Happy marriage—a long conversation that always seems too short.

☆　　　　☆　　　　☆

Henpecked husband—one who gives his wife the best ears of his life.

☆　　　　☆　　　　☆

High heels—the invention of a woman who had been kissed on the forehead.

☆　　　　☆　　　　☆

Hollywood marriage—a rest period between romances.

☆　　　　☆　　　　☆

Honeymoon—the vacation a man takes before beginning work under a new boss.

☆　　　　☆　　　　☆

Housewarming—last call for wedding presents.

☆　　　☆　　　☆

Hug—roundabout expression of affection.

☆　　　☆　　　☆

Husband—a man of few words.

☆　　　☆　　　☆

Husband—a man for whom the bills toll.

☆　　　☆　　　☆

Insanity—grounds for divorce in some states; grounds for marriage in all.

☆　　　☆　　　☆

Joy of motherhood—what a woman experiences when all the kids are in bed.

☆　　　☆　　　☆

Liberty—what a man exchanges for a wife.

☆　　　☆　　　☆

Lipstick—something which merely adds color and flavor to an old pastime.

☆　　　☆　　　☆

Married man—one who has two hands with which to steer a car.

☆　　　　☆　　　　☆

Married man—a guy who always turns off the motor when his wife calls, "I'll be right out."

☆　　　　☆　　　　☆

Matrimony—the only union which permits a woman to work unlimited overtime without extra pay.

☆　　　　☆　　　　☆

Model husband—always some other woman's.

☆　　　　☆　　　　☆

Monologue—a conversation being carried on by a man and his wife.

☆　　　　☆　　　　☆

Proposal—an attempt to acquire a huge vocabulary.

☆　　　　☆　　　　☆

Reno—where the honeymoon express is finally uncoupled.

☆　　　　☆　　　　☆

Reno—a large inland seaport in America with the tide running in and the untied running out.

☆   ☆   ☆

Rice—a product associated with the worst mistake of some men's life.

☆   ☆   ☆

Shotgun wedding—a case of wife or death.

☆   ☆   ☆

Smart man—one who keeps his eyes wide open before marriage and half-shut afterward.

☆   ☆   ☆

Wedding ring—a one-man band.

☆   ☆   ☆

Yawn—nature's way of letting a husband open his mouth.

☆   ☆   ☆

Yes-man—someone who is married.

☆   ☆   ☆

· 17 ·

Questions and Answers

Q: Can you take dictation?
A: No, I've never been married.

☆   ☆   ☆

Q: Why is a roomful of married people empty?
A: Because there is not a single person in it.

☆   ☆   ☆

Q: Why do women seek husbands named William?
A: So they can have a Will of their own.

☆   ☆   ☆

Q: What is the greatest water power
        known to a man?
A: Women's tears.

☆   ☆   ☆

Q: What word do women favor the
        most?
A: The last one.

☆   ☆   ☆

Q: What do they call someone who
        helps dad with the dishes?
A: The ideal wife.

☆   ☆   ☆

A: What is the difference between a
        lover and his rival?
Q: One kisses the miss, and the other
        misses the kiss.

☆   ☆   ☆

Q: Why is a newspaper like a wife?
A: Because every man should have one
        of his own and not look at his
        neighbor's.

☆   ☆   ☆

Q: What's the best way to find out
        what a woman thinks of you?

A: Marry her.

☆   ☆   ☆

Q: At what age is a man usually ready to get married?

A: At the parsonage.

☆   ☆   ☆

Q: What kind of husband do you think I should look for?

A: Better leave the husbands alone and look for a single man.

☆   ☆   ☆

Q: Who can stay single even if he married many women?

A: A minister.

☆   ☆   ☆

Q: What is a childish game?

A: One at which your wife beats you.

☆   ☆   ☆

Little boy: "Did you hear about the 88-year-old man and the 79-year-old lady that got married last week?"

Little girl: "Did they throw rice at them?"

Little boy: "No, they threw vitamins."

☆   ☆   ☆

His young son, studying geography, asked him,
"What do you call those people who wear rings
in their noses?"
"Husbands," he replied.

☆   ☆   ☆

· 18 ·

It Takes Two to Tango

Husband: "Don't put that money in your mouth—there's germs on it."

Wife: "Don't be silly—even a germ can't live on the money you earn."

☆　　　☆　　　☆

Melba: "I can't decide whether to go to a palmist or a mind-reader."

Ken: "Go to a palmist. It's obvious that you have a palm."

☆　　　☆　　　☆

Peggy: "You think so much of your old golf game you don't even remember when we were married."

Lowell: "Of course I do, my dear; it was the day I sank that 30-foot putt."

☆   ☆   ☆

He: "By the way, do you remember the time I made such an idiot out of myself?"
She: "Which time?"

☆   ☆   ☆

Wife: "I just got back from the beauty shop."
Husband: "What's the matter? Was it closed?"

☆   ☆   ☆

"But, my dear," protested the henpecked husband, "I've done nothing. You've been talking for an hour-and-a-half and I haven't said a word."
"I know," the wife replied. "But you listen like a wiseguy."

☆   ☆   ☆

Larry: "I don't look 38, do I?"
Judy: "Not anymore!"

☆   ☆   ☆

Nancy: "When I got on the bus, three men got up to give me their seats."

Buck: "Did you take them?"

☆   ☆   ☆

Dan: "Did you see that young lady smile
        at me?"
Karen: "That's nothing. The first time I
        saw you, I laughed right out loud."

☆   ☆   ☆

Wife: "You rat! Before we were married,
            you told me you were well off!"
Husband: "I was, but I didn't realize how well
            off."

☆   ☆   ☆

Ken: "You accuse me of reckless ex-
        travagance. When did I ever make a
        useless purchase?"
Melba: "Why, there's that fire extinguisher
        you bought a year ago. We've never
        used it once."

☆   ☆   ☆

Patty: "That's a beautiful rainbow tie
        you're wearing."
David: "What do you mean by a 'rainbow
        tie'?"
Patty: "It has a big pot at the end."

☆   ☆   ☆

Him: "When I stand on my head, the blood rushes to it. Why doesn't it rush to my feet when I stand up?"

Her: "That's because your feet aren't empty."

☆   ☆   ☆

Bill: "What do you mean by telling everyone I'm deaf and dumb?"

Sharon: "That's not true. I never said you were deaf."

☆   ☆   ☆

Bill: "I've had to make a living by my wits."

Gill: "Well, half a living is better than none."

☆   ☆   ☆

Bob: "Something came into my mind just now and went away again."

Esther: "Maybe it was lonely."

☆   ☆   ☆

Wife: "How many times have I told you not to be late for dinner?"

Husband: "I don't know. I thought you were keeping score."

☆   ☆   ☆

Wife: "This traffic jam is terrible. What shall I do?"

Husband: "I don't know, but I'm sure if you climb into the back seat you can figure it out."

☆　　　　☆　　　　☆

Angry wife to husband: "No! Every time we discuss something sensibly, I lose!"

☆　　　　☆　　　　☆

Wife: "Honey, will you still love me after I put on a few pounds?"

Husband: "Yes, I do."

☆　　　　☆　　　　☆

Don: "I simply can't bear idiots!"

Myrlene: "How odd—apparently your mother could."

☆　　　　☆　　　　☆

Wife: "At least you could talk to me while I sew."

Husband: "Why don't you sew to me while I read?"

☆　　　　☆　　　　☆

Wife: "The maid just quit. She said you spoke insultingly to her on the phone."

Husband: "Good heavens! I thought I was talk-
           ing to you!"

☆   ☆   ☆

Russ: "Now that looks like a happily mar-
           ried couple."
Amy: "Don't be too sure, my dear.
           They're probably saying the same
           thing about us."

☆   ☆   ☆

Wife: "Before we were married, we didn't
           sit this far apart in the car."
Husband: "Well, dear, I didn't move."

☆   ☆   ☆

Wife: "When we were younger, you used
           to nibble on my ear."
           (Husband starts to leave the room.)
Wife: "Where are you going?"
Husband: "To get my teeth!"

☆   ☆   ☆

Patty: "I had to marry you to find out how
           stupid you are."
Roy: "You should have known that the
           minute I asked you."

☆   ☆   ☆

Wife: "Scientists claim that the average person speaks 10,000 words a day."

Husband: "Yes, dear, but remember, you are far above average."

☆　　　☆　　　☆

Wife: "Are you positive you'll love me after I get ugly and old?"

Husband: "Who says I don't?"

☆　　　☆　　　☆

Wife: "I got this girdle today for a ridiculous figure."

Husband: "I know, but how much did it cost?"

☆　　　☆　　　☆

Wife: "Why do you go on the balcony when I sing? Don't you like to hear me?"

Husband: "I want the neighbors to see I'm not beating my wife."

☆　　　☆　　　☆

- 19 -

Divorce

Some people marry for love, and some for money, but most of them for only a short time.

☆   ☆   ☆

Divorce is the hash made from domestic scraps.

☆   ☆   ☆

When a neighbor told her she was getting a divorce from the meanest, crossest man in the world, she scoffed, "How can you get a divorce from my husband?"

☆   ☆   ☆

One woman I know charged her husband with mental cruelty so severe it caused her to lose 30 pounds. "Divorce granted!" said the judge. "Oh, not yet," the woman pleaded. "First I want to lose another 10 pounds."

☆   ☆   ☆

Marriage originates when a man meets the only woman who really understands him; so does divorce.

☆   ☆   ☆

Judging by the divorce rate, a lot of people who said "I do"—don't.

☆   ☆   ☆

The divorce rate would be lower if, instead of marrying for better or worse, people would marry for good.

☆   ☆   ☆

If people didn't get married for such silly reasons, they wouldn't get divorced for such silly reasons.

☆   ☆   ☆

Some people want a divorce right after their "mirage."

☆   ☆   ☆

Divorce records show that many married couples spend too much time in court and not enough time courting.

☆   ☆   ☆

About all that is necessary for a divorce nowadays is a wedding.

☆   ☆   ☆

With as many divorces as we have nowadays, it seems that more parents are running away from home than children.

☆   ☆   ☆

Seems like people nowadays get married before they know each other—and get divorced when they do.

☆   ☆   ☆

Most divorces are based on incompatibility, or at least the first two syllables of the word.

☆   ☆   ☆

The best way to decrease the number of divorces is for folks to stay divorced.

☆   ☆   ☆

A couple in Hollywood got divorced, then got remarried. The divorce didn't work out.

☆　　　☆　　　☆

Divorce has become so common that some folks are staying married just to be different.

☆　　　☆　　　☆

Divorce is quite useless. One gets married for lack of judgment. Then one gets divorced for lack of patience. And finally one remarries for lack of memory.

☆　　　☆　　　☆

His wife got rid of 235 pounds of ugly fat—she divorced him.

☆　　　☆　　　☆

Hollywood divorce—one in which the wife is asking for custody of the money.

☆　　　☆　　　☆

Judge:　　"You say you want a divorce because your husband is careless about his appearance?"

Wife:　　"That's right, judge. He hasn't shown up in almost two years."

☆　　　☆　　　☆

- 20 -

Overheard at the Marriage Counselor's Office

Men think women cannot be trusted too far.
Women think men can't be trusted too near.

☆   ☆   ☆

A man always chases a woman until she catches
him.

☆   ☆   ☆

A good husband is one who feels his pockets
every time he passes a mailbox.

☆   ☆   ☆

The wife who drives from the back seat isn't
any worse than the husband who cooks from the
dining-room table.

☆   ☆   ☆

Many a man loses his voice on his wedding day.

☆   ☆   ☆

The first year is the paper anniversary. After one year you're beaten to a pulp.

☆   ☆   ☆

Smart husband—one who thinks twice before saying nothing.

☆   ☆   ☆

A man laughs at a woman who puts on eyebrow makeup, but he spends ten minutes trying to comb two hairs across a bald spot.

☆   ☆   ☆

Some women court trouble while others just go right ahead and get married.

☆   ☆   ☆

The average bride gets enough advice to last for several husbands.

☆   ☆   ☆

You can't always judge how expensive a thing is by its price. The marriage license costs only a few bucks.

☆ ☆ ☆

One way to find out what a woman really thinks of you is to marry her.

☆ ☆ ☆

A man who thinks he is more intelligent than his wife is married to a smart woman!

☆ ☆ ☆

The modern husband believes a woman's place is in the home—and expects her to go there immediately after work.

☆ ☆ ☆

Were it not for imagination, a man would be just as happy with one girl as with any other.

☆ ☆ ☆

Feminine psychology—being smart enough to ask your husband's advice, but not dumb enough to take it.

☆ ☆ ☆

A modest girl never pursues a man, nor does a mousetrap pursue a mouse.

☆ ☆ ☆

Politicians and bridegrooms have one thing in common—they both forget their campaign promises.

☆   ☆   ☆

A girl who thinks marriage is the end of her education has a lot to learn.

☆   ☆   ☆

Successful marriages are based on two books—the cookbook and the checkbook.

☆   ☆   ☆

Modern marriage—to love, honor, and have children that disobey.

☆   ☆   ☆

Marriage—an investment that pays you dividends if you pay interest.

☆   ☆   ☆

With some marriages, holy wedlock becomes holy deadlock.

☆   ☆   ☆

Problems in marriage are often caused by a man showing his worst side to his better half.

☆ ☆ ☆

Comedians make light of marriage, but it has been proved that married life is healthy. Statistics show that single people die sooner than married folks. So if you're looking for a long life and a slow death, get married.

☆ ☆ ☆

On the Sea of Matrimony, many a dreamboat becomes a battleship.

☆ ☆ ☆

It's her second marriage, and now she has a new louse on life.

☆ ☆ ☆

A little common sense would prevent most divorces—and marriages, too.

☆ ☆ ☆

Don't marry for money; you can borrow it cheaper.

☆ ☆ ☆

Troubles come in doubles; that's why marriage requires two people.

☆ ☆ ☆

A man's successes are more likely to come if he has a wife to brag to about them.

☆   ☆   ☆

Modern fiction runs too much to love, and modern love runs too much to fiction.

☆   ☆   ☆

When a girl marries, she gives up the attentions of several men for the inattention of one.

☆   ☆   ☆

The misunderstood husband is the one whose wife understands him too well.

☆   ☆   ☆

It's a trial marriage—nothing could be more of a trial.

☆   ☆   ☆

Every argument has two sides, and they are usually married to each other.

☆   ☆   ☆

Fewer people would have trouble with their wedlock if they would remember the combination.

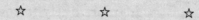

The new version of the modern triangle is: the husband, the wife, and the loan company.

☆   ☆   ☆

A man is never so weak as when some woman is telling him how strong he is.

☆   ☆   ☆

A good woman inspires a man, a brilliant woman interests him, a beautiful woman fascinates him—but a sympathetic woman gets him.

☆   ☆   ☆

What becomes of all those love triangles? Most of them turn into wrecktangles.

☆   ☆   ☆

You know it's a fact that it takes horse sense and stable thinking to stay hitched these days.

☆   ☆   ☆

A lot of marriage ties are cut by a sharp tongue.

☆   ☆   ☆

This country will never adopt polygamy. The divorce courts couldn't stand the strain.

☆ ☆ ☆

They're inseparable; it takes several people to pull them apart.

☆ ☆ ☆

They're very compatible. They both dislike each other.

☆ ☆ ☆

Before marriage, he talks and she listens; during the honeymoon, she talks and he listens; later they both talk and the neighbors listen.

☆ ☆ ☆

Many married couples manage to patch up their old quarrels until they are as good as new ones.

☆ ☆ ☆

One marriage in every five ends in divorce, but the other four couples fight it out to the bitter end.

☆ ☆ ☆

They're so incompatible that they have nothing in common to fight about.

☆ ☆ ☆

The three stages of modern family life are matrimony, acrimony, and alimony.

☆　　　☆　　　☆

A girl can be scared to death by a mouse or a spider, but she's often too willing to take her chances with a wolf.

☆　　　☆　　　☆

Nowadays two can live as cheaply as one if both are working.

☆　　　☆　　　☆

The U.S.A. is the only country where a housewife hires a woman to do her cleaning so she can do volunteer work at the day nursery where the cleaning woman leaves her child.

☆　　　☆　　　☆

Successful marriage—one in which the husband knows when to remember and the wife knows what to forget.

☆　　　☆　　　☆

Two can live as cheaply as one if one doesn't eat.

☆　　　☆　　　☆

It's better to be laughed at for not being married

than to be unable to laugh because you are.

☆   ☆   ☆

And speaking about all these marriages of high-school kids, one elderly gent of 20 swore he attended one wedding ceremony where the bridegroom wept for two hours. It seems the bride got a bigger piece of cake than he did.

☆   ☆   ☆

We should all be very grateful to our neighbors. Just think—a marriage counselor gets $25 an hour to listen to a couple yelling and screaming and fighting. Neighbors do it for nothing.

☆   ☆   ☆

"Frankly, we only stay together because of the children. They're marriage counselors."

☆   ☆   ☆

The grave of their love was excavated with little digs.

☆   ☆   ☆

Their home is frequently closed for altercations.

☆   ☆   ☆

They get along like two peeves in a pod.

☆　　　　☆　　　　☆

"You say you love me," she tells him. "If you really did, why didn't you marry someone else?"

☆　　　　☆　　　　☆

She keeps saying, "Tell me again what a good married life we're having—I keep forgetting."

☆　　　　☆　　　　☆

The husband and wife took their six children to the marriage counselor. "Our marriage would have broken up if it weren't for the children," she explained. "My husband won't take them, and I won't take them."

☆　　　　☆　　　　☆

A lawyer complained to the marriage counselor that the reason his marriage was going on the rocks was because his wife was so immature. "Would you believe it? Every time I take a bath, she comes in and sinks all my boats!"

☆　　　　☆　　　　☆

Wife:　　　"We have been married five years and haven't agreed on a thing."
Husband:　"You're wrong again—it has been six years."

☆　　　　☆　　　　☆

"We sleep in separate rooms, we have dinner apart, we take separate vacations—we're doing everything we can to keep our marriage together."

☆　　　☆　　　☆

"Mr. Marriage Counselor, what can I do to help my husband get over his inferiority complex? I keep telling him he is terrific and smart and handsome, but he doesn't believe me."
"Do you think the fact that I have asked for a divorce has shaken his confidence?"

☆　　　☆　　　☆

Marriage counselor to his wife: "Maybe your problem is that you've been waking up grumpy in the morning."
Wife: "No, I always let him sleep."

☆　　　☆　　　☆

Wife: "My husband frightens me the way he blows smoke rings through his nose."
Psychiatrist: "That isn't unusual."
Wife: "But my husband doesn't smoke."

☆　　　☆　　　☆

"What do you think of trial marriages?"
"I must be frank—all marriages are trial marriages."

☆   ☆   ☆

Wife: "My husband thinks he's a
             refrigerator."
Psychiatrist: "I wouldn't worry as long as he's
             not violent."
Wife: "Oh, the delusion doesn't bother
             me. But when he sleeps with his
             mouth open the little light keeps me
             awake."

☆   ☆   ☆

Marriage counselor: "Do you feel that your role
             as a mother and homemaker is
             beneath you?"
Counselee: "No, I feel it's beyond me."

☆   ☆   ☆

Marriage counselor: "Do you encourage your
             husband in his work?"
Counselee: "I do my best. I keep telling him he
ought to ask for a raise."

☆   ☆   ☆

Marriage counselor: "Do you enjoy talking to
             each other?"
Counselee: "Oh, we enjoy talking to each other
             all right. The problem is listening to
             each other."

☆   ☆   ☆